EVEREST

Reaching the Roof of the World

ALSO BY DAVID LONG ...

Survival in Space:
The Apollo 13 Mission

Tragedy at Sea:
The Sinking of the Titanic

Tutankhamun's Treasure:
Discovering the Secret Tomb of
Egypt's Ancient King

EVEREST

Reaching the Roof of the World

DAVID LONG

Illustrated by
STEFANO TAMBELLINI

Barrington Stoke

First published in 2022 in Great Britain by
Barrington Stoke Ltd
18 Walker Street, Edinburgh, EH3 7LP

www.barringtonstoke.co.uk

A CIP catalogue record for this book is available
from the British Library upon request

ISBN: 978-1-80090-094-3

Printed by Hussar Books, Poland

For university friends.
PER ARDUA AD ALTA

Contents

1

WHY EVEREST?

Everest is the world's highest mountain, reaching 8,849 metres above sea level. It has attracted great interest from people around the world for more than 100 years. This isn't surprising. Mount Everest towers like a huge icy giant over the Himalayas – an enormous mountain range in Asia that's more than 2,000 kilometres long.

The Himalayas stretches over six countries: China, India, Bhutan, Nepal, Tibet and Pakistan.

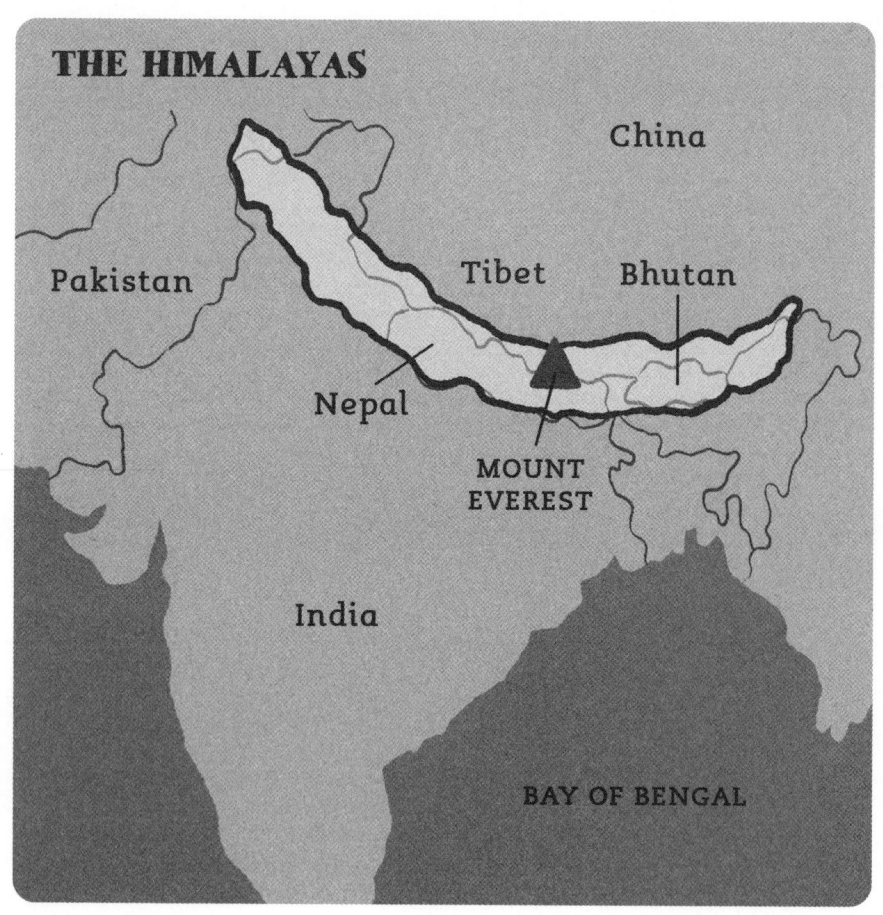

THE HIMALAYAS

China

Pakistan

Tibet

Bhutan

Nepal

MOUNT
EVEREST

India

BAY OF BENGAL

The area has always been a magical place for the millions of people living nearby. Ancient stories and legends about the mountains are important in their religious lives. In Tibet they call the highest peak of the Himalayas Chomolungma, meaning "Goddess Mother of the World". The Nepali word, Sagarmatha, means "Peak of Heaven".

The English name, Mount Everest, is more famous than the other names but nowhere near as old. It only dates back to Victorian times, when much of Asia was part of the British Empire. Many of those who lived in and around the Himalayas were ruled by Great Britain, and an official from London called George Everest was in India producing new maps that were more accurate than before.

There were so many huge mountains in the Himalayas that no one could tell which was the highest. It took until 1852 for the correct one to be identified, by a talented Indian mathematician called Radhanath Sikdar.

For a while this highest point was just shown on maps as "Peak B" or "Peak XV". But then someone suggested renaming it after George Everest.

George said no to the idea as soon as he heard it. He had never set foot on this mountain or even seen it from a distance. At this time it is unlikely that any Europeans had been near the mountain, and George Everest was worried that the people living in the region would find this new name difficult to pronounce.

Others did want George's surname to be used, however, and so it was given to the mighty mountain. Everest is still the name used most around the world today, but the people living in the Himalayas don't often refer to it this way.

There was a lot more interest in the mountain after it had been identified as the highest peak on Earth. The nineteenth and early twentieth centuries were important times for science and discovery. Explorers and adventurers risked their lives as they travelled thousands of kilometres up great rivers like the Nile and the Amazon. Others attempted to walk to the North and South Poles across the vast frozen wastelands. Some explorers trekked over the awfully hot, dry deserts of Asia and Africa in search of ancient cities.

Some of the most determined adventurers were also keen mountain climbers – mountaineers. Rock climbing was a fairly new sport, but it had become very popular, especially in Britain. Climbers had already reached the highest and hardest European peaks by the time Mount Everest was given its new name. The best mountaineers were looking for new and more exciting challenges at the beginning of the twentieth century.

The Himalayas looked like the perfect place to test their skills and their courage. This part of Asia is home to nine of the world's ten highest peaks. Even the relatively small mountains in the Himalayas are hundreds or thousands of metres taller than anything in Europe and America.

For example, the Matterhorn on the border between Italy and Switzerland is one of the most famous mountains in Europe – and the hardest to climb. Hundreds of people have died trying to reach the summit. Yet the Matterhorn is only about half the height of Mount Everest, at 4,478 metres.

Mount Everest stretches nearly five and
a half miles high – almost nine kilometres.
Planes fly around this high, far above the
clouds. It's easy to see why the mountaineers
began to find something magical about the
mountain too, just like the locals, but for them
it had nothing to do with religion.

The mountaineers wanted to reach places
no one else had reached before and achieve
something nobody else had achieved. The
difficulty and dangers of such a long climb
made Everest more exciting to them than any
other mountain. They wanted to stand on what
had become known as "the roof of the world".

MOUNTAINS OF THE WORLD

Mount Everest: 8,849m
NEPAL AND TIBET

The highest mountain
in the world

Aconcagua: 6,961m
ARGENTINA, S.AMERICA

The highest mountain in
the western hemisphere

Mount Kilimanjaro: 5,895m
TANZANIA, AFRICA

The highest mountain in Africa

Commercial planes: 11,000m

9,000 metres

8,000 metres

Matterhorn: 4,478m
SWITZERLAND AND ITALY, EUROPE

The highest mountain in Europe

7,000 metres

Mount Fuji: 3,776m
JAPAN, ASIA

The highest mountain in Japan

6,000 metres

5,000 metres

4,000 metres

3,000 metres

2,000 metres

Mount Snowdon: 1,085m
WALES, UK

The mountain on which
Hunt and his team trained

1,000 metres

0 metres

2

TRYING BUT FAILING

The view from the roof of the world can be amazing. On a clear day, it is possible to see more than 300 kilometres in every direction from the peak of Everest. But conditions there are hardly ever perfect, and for most of the year the weather makes it impossible to climb to the summit.

Even in the spring the weather can be terrifying on the lower slopes, and it gets much worse closer to the top. The wind can blow at speeds of more than 250 kilometres per hour at the top. Snowfalls, ice and avalanches are deadly hazards for even the most experienced mountaineers on the way up.

Also, temperatures in the Himalayas sometimes plunge to 40 degrees below zero (or worse). The climbers attempting to reach the summit of Everest in the nineteenth century had none of the protective gear that mountaineers wear today. They wore only leather boots and ordinary wool and cotton clothes.

Everest's immense height also makes breathing very difficult. At 8,000 metres, the air contains only a third of the oxygen most

EARLY MOUNTAINEER **MODERN-DAY CLIMBER**

of us are used to. Climbers call this the "death zone". The idea of climbing to such a height must have seemed impossible when the first British mountaineer arrived in the Himalayas in the 1880s.

He was called William Graham, and he didn't even try climbing Everest. However, it is believed he reached several of the smaller peaks. No one is sure which peaks these were because the local maps weren't very good and the notes William Graham made are confusing. He had several setbacks too, including when his leather boots caught alight while he was drying them over a campfire. But his exciting adventures encouraged others to follow his example, and more mountaineers began making the long, expensive journey to the Himalayas.

The first serious attempt by these mountaineers to climb Everest took place around a hundred years ago. In 1921 a British team trekked to the foot of the mountain. They were the first Europeans to get this far, but the team's doctor had a heart attack and died on the way. A year later someone from the team came back as part of a larger expedition – school teacher George Mallory. This time he wanted to climb Everest from the north side, but he couldn't decide if he should take oxygen cylinders to use when he got up high.

The cylinders were made of metal and very heavy, but Mallory knew a lack of oxygen could badly affect his strength and stamina.

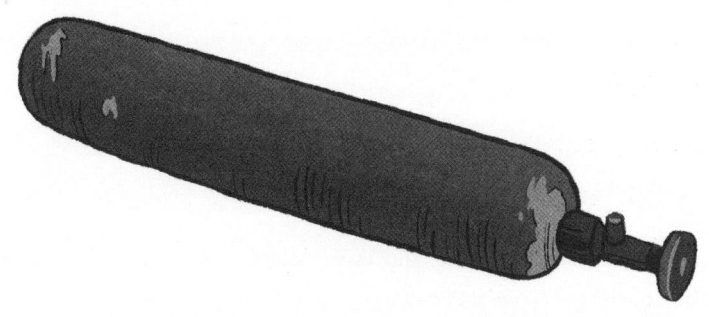

Climbers lacking oxygen can also find it hard to focus, which makes accidents much more likely. But some mountaineers think it's cheating to carry oxygen and that it is possible to get used to the thin air. This is called acclimatisation – when someone stops and rests a lot on the way up, often for days or weeks at a time.

Everest is much too high to climb in one go, even with oxygen. This means an expedition always involves setting up a series of camps along the mountainside to use for eating and sleeping. These have to include tents, sleeping bags, food and first-aid supplies, and equipment for cooking and climbing – such as lightweight ladders for crossing crevasses. Only a few people at a time will attempt to reach the summit from the highest camp, and they take it in turns to see who can get there first.

When it was Mallory's turn to head for the summit, he and his three companions decided to try without oxygen. Three of them reached 8,230 metres despite the increased dangers, before turning back to camp. Getting to this height set an exciting new world record, but they were too cold and too exhausted to go any higher.

Another two climbers tried to reach the summit four days later. This time they took oxygen with them, believing that the benefits of the gas would make up for the extra weight of the cylinders. They had to shelter for a day and two nights in the death zone because of a terrible storm. But when the wind dropped slightly, they were able to climb even higher than Mallory had managed. One of them, George Finch, reached 8,326 metres, another record.

A third group, including Mallory, went afterwards, again taking oxygen. But this time disaster struck. The climbers were hit by an avalanche, and nine men were swept over the edge of an ice cliff. Mallory was knocked 45 metres down the mountainside and buried under deep snow. Luckily he wasn't badly injured, but seven other members of the team were killed.

This tragedy meant the expedition had to be stopped, but Mallory was determined to try again. He returned to Everest in 1924 as part of a team of hardened, experienced climbers.

They included a photographer whose job was to take pictures of what everyone hoped would be a successful climb to the summit at last.

Three separate attempts were made to reach the summit. The first one failed due to bad weather, but another record was set during the second try. This time a climber called Edward Norton managed to reach 8,565 metres. He knew he was close to the summit, but he felt too exhausted to go any further. Also, his climbing partner had become terribly ill and nearly died. Both of them were worried about how much time they had left before it got dark.

The pair slowly limped back down to the camp. Mallory decided to make a final attempt two days later with a student called Andrew Irvine. This time they agreed to carry oxygen and food that would last them for a day's hard climbing. But what happened next is still one of the greatest mysteries in the history of mountaineering.

The weather was good for the Himalayas, and the mood in the camp was cheerful and positive. The climbers left behind had a telescope, and some of the time they could see Mallory and Irvine a long way off in the distance. They looked like two tiny dots on the huge misty mountain.

The camp last saw Mallory and Irvine through the telescope around lunchtime two days later when the mist briefly cleared. But after this they weren't ever seen alive again. A search party went out to look for them but found nothing. Mallory's body wasn't discovered until 75 years later. The remains had been picked over by giant black ravens – one of the few birds that flies this high. Irvine's body has never been found. No one knows if one of them managed to reach the summit of Everest before dying.

3

RACE FOR THE TOP

Two of the expeditions involving George
Mallory had ended in tragedy despite being
well planned and carefully organised. Not
everyone did it this way, however.

The strangest attempt to reach the summit of Everest was by a man from Yorkshire called Maurice Wilson. He had almost no experience of mountaineering and only a few flying lessons when he decided to pilot a small plane nearly 8,000 kilometres from Britain to Tibet.

Wilson's plan was to crash-land on the upper slopes of Mount Everest and then walk the rest of the way to the top on his own. The old Gipsy Moth biplane he'd bought hadn't cost very much money and wasn't very good. He crashed it the first time he tried taking off from England. But Wilson didn't give up and had the plane repaired as cheaply as possible. He was then told by the Air Ministry he wasn't allowed to fly to Tibet, but this just made him even more determined to go.

Wilson somehow managed to reach India without crashing again. But he was ordered to fly back to England. When he said he wouldn't, the Indian authorities took away the biplane.

Wilson just shrugged, picked up his backpack and started to walk the several hundred kilometres to the foot of Mount Everest.

Now his problems really began. Wilson had no climbing skills, was wearing the wrong clothing and had none of the right equipment.

He kept a diary describing how he was stopped by bad weather five days into the climb. Wilson tried again after resting for a few days, but once again he had to stop and find shelter because of the appalling weather. The weather finally improved, but then Wilson found his path to the top was blocked by a solid wall of ice more than ten metres high.

He had no idea how to climb up ice, so he decided to try a different route, but his luck had run out. The last words written in his diary were cheery ones – "Off again, gorgeous day" – but Maurice Wilson didn't get very far. His body was discovered by another climber a year later, frozen stiff, and his diary was brought back to London.

*

Mountaineering had been a mostly British hobby up until that point. British climbers were the first to use special ropes and ice

axes, and the British had successfully climbed more European peaks before anyone else. But by the 1930s the race to climb the world's highest mountains was becoming much more international.

Many adventurers wanted to succeed on behalf of their countries. Explorers from Italy and Norway had reached both the North and South Poles. Two Frenchmen had driven a Citroen car more than 3,000 kilometres across the Sahara Desert (and back again!). An American called Wiley Post had flown around the world alone. Everest was beginning to look like the last real challenge left for anyone who wanted to plant their country's flag somewhere no one else had been before.

American, German, Russian and Swiss climbers began travelling to the mountainous regions of Asia to try to reach the top of Everest. In 1933 the British millionaire Lucy Houston paid for a Royal Air Force pilot to fly right over the summit. Squadron Leader Lord Clydesdale used a bomber aircraft fitted with new heaters, oxygen tanks and a special camera.

The flight was difficult and very dangerous because propellers don't work well in thin air. But the photographs taken were fantastically detailed, and they were used to identify new routes up the mountain for future expeditions.

*

The next three attempts to reach the summit were unsuccessful, and then the Second World War prevented any further travel to the Himalayas between 1939 and 1945.

The first person to try to summit Everest after the war was a Canadian in 1947. But he reached only 6,700 metres before deciding to give up and go home. A team of British and American climbers had no more success in 1950. A year after that a Danish climber had to turn back because of a heavy rockfall.

These three expeditions were fairly small, sometimes no more than two or three people, and many of the climbers were not very experienced. Some were also badly prepared – such as the two people who hoped to survive by eating cheese and using a small candle to melt snow for drinking water.

There had now been at least twelve failed attempts and sixteen deaths. People must have started to wonder if anyone would reach the summit of Everest. By 1952 no one had got higher than 8,598 metres, but the best mountaineers still wanted to keep trying. That year the largest team so far began making preparations for yet another go.

The team's official name was the British Mount Everest Expedition, and it was led by a senior officer in the British Army. But the members were from all over the world. The people who would be climbing came from England, Wales and New Zealand. They would be relying on the support of a huge team of local guides and helpers from India and Nepal.

4

FIRST WALES THEN NEPAL

In 1952 the expedition leader, Colonel John Hunt, gathered together a team of keen, experienced climbers. This included soldiers and scientists as well as two doctors, a schoolmaster, a film-maker, a wartime code-breaker and a beekeeper. When winter arrived, they began training in a mountainous region of Wales called Snowdonia.

The summit of Mount Snowdon is the highest point in the area, yet only reaches 1,085 metres. But Wales has some of the worst weather in Europe. This creates

challenges when climbing, such as slippery, crumbling rock faces, which makes it very popular with mountaineers. George Mallory visited Snowdonia several times. His partner Andrew Irvine once rode a motorbike nearly a thousand metres up the side of another local peak called Foel Grach.

Snowdon's steepest cliff is nicknamed "Cloggy" and is one of the hardest to climb in the whole of Britain. Colonel John Hunt thought it and the slippery rocks of the nearby Glyderau peaks would be perfect for improving his team's climbing skills. Spending time in Wales would give everyone an opportunity to get used to working together. They could also test the latest oxygen breathing equipment and learn how to use it properly.

The climbers spent several months in Snowdonia, training hard during the day and staying overnight at the Royal Hotel in the village of Capel Curig. Today this hotel is called Pen-Y-Gwryd and is run by a mountaineering charity. Visitors can still see the signatures of Hunt and his team, who wrote their names on the ceiling during their stay.

By February 1953 the team's training was complete. It was time to pack up and leave. Hunt arranged for the climbers to travel to Tilbury in Essex, where most of them boarded a steamship called the *Stratheden*. This would be sailing for India, and it gave the mountaineers their last chance for several months to eat proper food and sleep in a comfortable bed. The rest of the team travelled to India by plane, which was faster but much more expensive.

Expeditions like this need a huge amount of planning. Whichever route is used, climbing from the foot of Everest to the summit takes weeks not days. This requires masses of equipment and supplies, far more than the climbers can carry on their backs.

Everything had to be transported nearly 300 kilometres from the Nepalese capital of

Kathmandu to the bottom of Everest before any climbing could begin. With no railways and very few roads, this was a big challenge for Hunt and his team. Their supplies and equipment had to be carried by hand and transported on foot.

Once this had been done, there was the problem of how to get everything up the mountain. The team needed suitable sites for the camps leading up to the summit. All the tents and other supplies would have to be carried up to each new camp from the one below.

This would mean the mountaineers could climb gradually from one camp to the next. They could rest at each camp before pushing on to the next one, which would be the best way for the climbers to get used to the thin atmosphere. The camps would also give them somewhere to shelter at night or in an emergency – for example, when one of Everest's famous storms blew up.

Hunt had worked all this out before leaving England. His plan was for the first camp, known as base camp, to be set up at around 5,500 metres. If the weather was all right, Hunt calculated that it would take several more weeks to set up six further camps in a line going up the mountain. The final camp would be at around 7,300 metres, which they'd reach around another two weeks after that.

Hunt would wait until then to decide which of the climbers would leave from the highest camp and attempt to reach the summit.

5

WHO ARE THE SHERPAS?

Hunt's 1953 expedition was the largest ever organised, but it was impossible for him and his twelve climbers to do everything on their own. They had several tonnes of food, clothing, special equipment, scientific instruments and fuel stored in Kathmandu. Together with the

heavy oxygen cylinders this would have filled
a large truck, but instead everything had to be
carried by hand to the foot of Mount Everest.

More than 300 local porters were hired to
help Hunt's team do this. Most of the porters
were Indian or Nepalese, but 20 were local men

known as Sherpas. This is the name given
to families who originally came from Tibet
but settled in Nepal. In the past, Sherpas
were nomadic, meaning they spent their lives
moving from place to place in search of food for
themselves and their yaks, which they bred for
meat, milk and skins.

Sherpas have lived in the Himalayas for thousands of years, and many have become excellent climbers. They are often employed as mountain guides and paid to help move supplies and equipment. Their huge experience and deep knowledge of the mountains means they continue to play a vital role in almost every expedition to the Himalayas today.

In recent years, Sherpas have broken many important world records. The person who has climbed Everest more than anyone else is a Sherpa named Kami Rita – he has reached the summit an incredible 26 times. The fastest ever climb to the summit was made by a Sherpa, and in 2005 a young Sherpa and his Nepalese girlfriend became the first people to get married at the summit. Sherpas have also saved the lives of countless other mountaineers. In 2013 a Sherpa carried out the world's highest ever rescue when an injured climber got stranded inside the death zone at over 8,500 metres.

None of this had happened by the time Hunt and his team were ready to leave Kathmandu, but Sherpas were already known for their toughness, skill and determination. They were also much better at coping with the thin air than other mountaineers, so it made sense for

Colonel Hunt to ask them to support this latest attempt on Everest. The 20 Sherpas included an energetic and smiley 38 year old called Tenzing Norgay. He already held the record for climbing higher than anyone else, after getting to 8,598 metres the previous year.

Hunt's first group of climbers and Sherpas left Bhadgaon near Kathmandu on 10 March with 180 porters to help carry the equipment 300 kilometres to the bottom of Mount Everest. The rest set off the following day, with their own group of porters, to begin the long and exhausting trek.

For the next eleven days or so both groups followed pretty much the same route into the mountains that an unsuccessful Swiss team had taken a year before. This narrow, winding track took them uphill and downhill, twisting and turning over a spectacular landscape of rice fields, jungle, green pine trees and gentle grassy meadows.

The weather here was mostly good, apart from one wild storm that suddenly blew up while the men were camped by a remote Buddhist monastery. They were forced to take shelter when thousands of hailstones as large as marbles pelted from the sky and a vicious wind threatened to batter their tents to the ground.

The storm cleared the following day, and they saw Everest looming in the distance, huge and terrifying. For the first time on the long trek individual details on the slopes were visible. They could see steep rock faces and a vast river of ice with jagged crevasses sliced into the surface like deep cuts. It looked exciting from this distance but also frightening.

The rocky path continued with dramatic twists and turns. It had so many zigzags that it took three more days for the team to trek just under thirty kilometres. They reached the chilly waters of the Dudh Kosi river and had to cut down several trees to make a log bridge across it. Seventeen days after leaving Bhadgaon they arrived at Thyangboche, a village near the foot of Everest.

Most of the porters dropped the supplies they'd been carrying, collected the money they had been promised and set off on the long, slow walk back to Kathmandu. Hunt and his team were now ready to begin acclimatising themselves to life in thin air and to prepare for their big climb.

6

EARTHQUAKES AND ICE FALLS

It had been demanding to spend nearly three weeks trekking hundreds of kilometres up from Kathmandu, but now the hard work really began.

Every previous expedition to Everest had failed, but they had each provided lots of useful information for the next group of climbers. Colonel Hunt had carefully studied every failure, and he was confident that his team was the best prepared so far.

His team also had the best, most modern equipment, but they still needed to find the right route up Everest. They spent the next eighteen days exploring different rocky ridges, glaciers and valleys to discover which route offered the best chance of success.

This process was slow and extremely time-consuming. The team spent whole days scrambling several kilometres over rocks, snow and ice. They would often climb up and down a different part of the mountain but then find it was a dead end or too dangerous to go any further. This was frustrating, but it was still good training, and it gave the climbers more time to acclimatise. Everyone was slowly getting used to climbing in thin air, but they were never as good at this as the Sherpas.

On 12 April Hunt was ready to begin setting up his new base camp at 5,455 metres. This meant several tonnes of equipment had to be carried up from Thyangboche to a height far greater than almost any European summit.

From base camp they had to find a way through the Khumbu Icefall, one of the most dangerous areas on Everest. In the 1920s George Mallory had said it was impossible to cross, and over the years many mountaineers had died trying to prove him wrong. One of them was hit by a falling block of ice the size of a twelve-storey building. More recently, in 2014, sixteen Nepalese climbers were killed (and nine very seriously injured) in a huge avalanche when tens of thousands of tonnes of snow and ice came crashing down the mountain.

The icefall is part of the Khumbu Glacier, a vast river of ice which slides down Everest at a rate of about a metre a day. It is the highest glacier in the world and stretches around seventeen kilometres from end to end.

Deep crevasses can suddenly open up in the glacier at any time, and climbers caught on its surface risk falling to their deaths. Towers of ice known as seracs are another constant danger. Often the size of large houses, seracs frequently break apart without warning and then plunge down the mountainside at high speed. The risk of this is worsened by the fact the Himalayas tend to get hit by violent earthquakes.

It took Hunt's team several days to find a route through the Khumbu Icefall, but they were lucky. They managed to cross it without injury, although one falling serac passed between a climber and a Sherpa. The serac was so close that they both felt it brush past.

Other problems began to emerge. Some
of the men were beginning to feel the effects
of altitude sickness as they climbed up the
Khumbu Glacier. This happens when a lack
of oxygen affects blood vessels in the brain.
Someone suffering from altitude sickness can
get terrible headaches and severe dizziness
which make it even harder for the climber to

focus. The result can be disastrous when even a small mistake can put an entire team in danger.

Snow-blindness was another growing issue. This is a temporary but very painful condition caused by bright sunlight reflecting off the snow. It feels a bit like having sunburnt eyes. Hunt's team solved it by putting sticky tape over the lenses of the men's goggles. The Sherpas had never seen this before and thought it looked very funny.

As well as these challenges, the climbers experienced the normal difficulties that all mountaineers face at such high altitudes. Natural snow and ice bridges that look solid can suddenly collapse. Ropes and other equipment can snap or fail. Heavy snowfalls for several hours every day make it almost impossible to spot any hidden dangers.

Despite all this, Hunt's advance camps were slowly put into place, each new one

slightly higher than the last. Camp II was set
up at 5,900 metres on 15 April. A week later
Camp III was established at 6,200 metres.
Nine days after that Camp IV was completed
at 6,400 metres.

THE SOUTH ROUTE

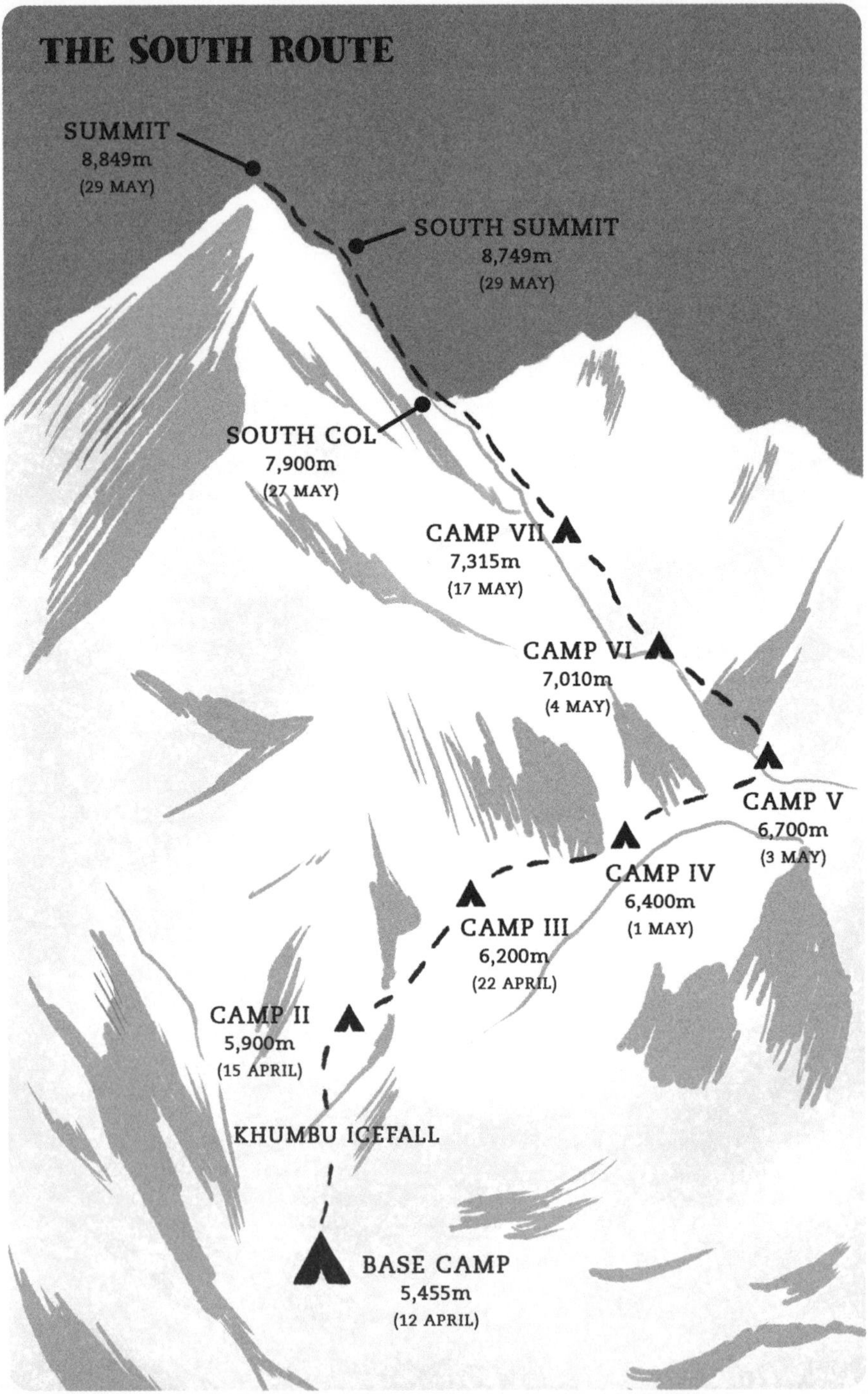

SUMMIT
8,849m
(29 MAY)

SOUTH SUMMIT
8,749m
(29 MAY)

SOUTH COL
7,900m
(27 MAY)

CAMP VII
7,315m
(17 MAY)

CAMP VI
7,010m
(4 MAY)

CAMP V
6,700m
(3 MAY)

CAMP IV
6,400m
(1 MAY)

CAMP III
6,200m
(22 APRIL)

CAMP II
5,900m
(15 APRIL)

KHUMBU ICEFALL

BASE CAMP
5,455m
(12 APRIL)

It took until 17 May for the seventh camp to be set up at 7,315 metres – over four and a half miles above sea level. To get this high had taken more than a month from base camp. That's not surprising when it's incredibly hard to find safe places to pitch a tent and hundreds of kilogrammes of gear must be carried up from one camp to the next.

Daily snowstorms had made the climb even harder, and even the Sherpas found it difficult to breathe at this altitude without using the oxygen equipment. But only one Sherpa failed to make it to the highest camp.

7

SO NEAR AND YET SO FAR

Hunt estimated that the team would be able to make just two or three attempts on the summit. After this, the weather would force everyone back down to Thyangboche.

Hunt knew from experience that May is the only good month for climbing at high altitude in the Himalayas. Any earlier than this and freezing temperatures make it almost impossible to survive. The mountain is also buffeted by fierce winds for weeks at a time, often as strong as 160 kilometres per hour – enough to kill or injure a climber in seconds.

The mountain warms up slightly after May, during the summer season. But this makes avalanches even more likely because when the snow starts to melt, it becomes even more unstable. Around 80 per cent of the rain on Everest falls during the summer too – July is the wettest month. Changes in air pressure also make it even harder to breathe at some times of the year than at others.

One of Hunt's trickiest tasks was deciding which of the climbers would be the most likely to reach the summit in the limited time they had left. Everyone in the team was good enough to be given a chance. They all wanted to be chosen – even those suffering from altitude sickness. The lucky pair were Tom Bourdillon, a rocket scientist, and Charles Evans, who was one of the team doctors.

Both had been mountaineering for years and had already taken part in several expeditions in Europe and Asia. Bourdillon had begun climbing as a young schoolboy. As an adult, he'd used his scientific knowledge to help his father invent the oxygen apparatus which he and Evans would be using.

A few days earlier they had managed to climb above 7,300 metres while trying to find a suitable route up to the summit. This is known as a "recce". But they had been beaten back by awful weather after finding large areas of soft, deep snow.

This snow came up to their thighs, and it is something mountaineers dread. Very deep

snow is exhausting to walk through even at
ground level, and in the mountains it means
avalanches are more likely.

Evans and Bourdillon were accompanied
by Hunt and three of the Sherpas to an area
known as the South Col. At 7,900 metres, this
was slightly below the death zone, but getting
there became a horrendous struggle.

A gale-force wind had been blowing for
two days. This was so strong that they had
difficulty just standing up. Everyone was soon

exhausted by the effort of climbing. They had to remove their oxygen masks so they could see what they were doing, but that made things even worse. The wind also meant it was nearly impossible to put up their small tents. It took more than an hour to get just one of them up because powerful gusts kept ripping the fabric and ropes out of the men's hands.

The weather can change very fast on Everest, and it was a miracle when the worst of the wind dropped away a few hours later. By the following morning there was just a very cold, stiff breeze. However, Bourdillon and Evans felt too tired to climb any further. One of the Sherpas was also sick, so it was decided to spend the day resting. Hunt trekked some distance along the South Col on his own, but the rest of the group relaxed as well as they could in this bleak and uncomfortable spot.

A day later the wind was blowing hard again and thick clouds were bubbling up from below. However, Bourdillon and Evans felt a bit better and set out for the summit early. They were delayed by a broken valve on one of the oxygen sets but fixed it and began inching their way further up the icy slope and into the death zone.

By 9 a.m. they had climbed to a height of almost 8,300 metres. There they came across an astonishing sight. In front of them were the broken remains of the tent used by Tenzing Norgay the year before. He had slept in this during his world-record climb with the Swiss. Now there was almost nothing left – just two bare poles sticking out of the snow and a few scraps of yellow cloth. The rest of the tent had been ripped apart by the wind and blown away.

The climb became even harder from this point onwards. Heavy snow fell onto a surface of loose, broken rocks – a dangerous combination that slowed Bourdillon and Evans down. They could only cover just over 100 metres an hour, and it took until 10.30 a.m. to reach 8,598 metres, matching Tenzing Norgay's record.

Swirling mist made it hard to see very far ahead, and the wind was growing stronger again. Bourdillon and Evans began to realise that they might not have enough time or enough oxygen to reach the top of Everest and get back down again.

But they kept moving slowly forward. By 1 p.m. they were standing at 8,749 metres on a spot called the South Summit. They had climbed higher than anyone had ever climbed before, and ahead of them they could see the actual summit. It was only a hundred metres further up, almost within reach, but they knew they had to turn back. They might have had enough oxygen to get up there, but it was bound to run out on the way down and this would kill them. The disappointment was enormous: their attempt had failed.

8

SUCCESS AT LAST

Bourdillon and Evans knew they had made the right decision, but getting back to camp was far from easy. The oxygen equipment used by Evans had broken again, and this time it couldn't be fixed. He was soon in a lot of pain. Both Evans and Bourdillon had got so cold and exhausted that an accident on the steep climb down from the South Summit seemed even more likely than it had done on the way up.

Somehow they made it back to the shelter of Camp VII, but only after several hours of hard trekking. The rest of the team celebrated their safe return and their spectacular new world record, but it was miserable to have got so far and then fail.

For the next attempt Hunt chose Edmund Hillary from New Zealand and Tenzing Norgay. They set off three days later, at six thirty in the morning, after an early breakfast of biscuits and tinned sardines. By nine o'clock they were already at the South Summit. They still had plenty of time and lots of oxygen, but both of them could see trouble ahead.

Everyone had hoped that the final stretch up to the summit would be a bit easier than the rest of the climb, but in fact the complete opposite was true. The most obvious obstacle was a rocky cliff more than twelve metres high. Climbing it looked impossible in these cold, wet conditions, but Hillary managed to struggle up to the top with Norgay's assistance. Hillary climbed up a large crack on one side of the cliff, between the rock and a frozen ridge of snow, and was then able to help Norgay up behind him.

They slumped in the snow for a short rest, feeling more confident about their chances of

success. They began working their way up the final slope, which meant finding a route past a series of humps beneath the snow. These humps went on and on, yet somehow the summit never seemed to get any closer.

After a while, Hillary began to wonder how long they could keep going, but then at around eleven thirty the ground seemed to flatten out and suddenly they were there. It was nearly a hundred years after Everest had been identified as the world's highest mountain, and now Hillary and Tenzing had finally made it to the top. The two men were standing on the roof of the world.

Mountaineers have always found it difficult to describe the experience of reaching a high summit after a really long climb. It's exciting and an incredible achievement, especially for the first people to do it. But it's never the end of the adventure. Climbing down a mountain can be as hard and as dangerous as climbing up it – or harder and even more dangerous if the climber is injured or exhausted. An expedition doesn't finish when climbers reach the top – only when everyone is safely back down.

Tenzing later described how he felt to reach the summit of Everest. He shook hands with Hillary and afterwards said it "was like meeting an old friend. You do not want to talk, but you are glad to be there." Tenzing and Hillary knew they had made history and that everyone in the team could be proud of their achievement. But they also knew that they needed to get down from the summit as fast as possible if they were to survive. The summer weather made the Khumbu Icefall more unstable and dangerous. All mountaineers know that more people die coming down Everest than going up it.

The men who finally conquered the "Peak of Heaven" only got to spend fifteen minutes at the summit after years of planning and training, and many hard months in the Himalayas.

Tenzing and Hillary removed their masks to save oxygen and shared some Kendal mint cake to regain some energy. They also took a handful of photographs and buried a few sweets and a small cross in the snow to show they had been there. But Hillary could already feel his movements becoming slow and clumsy. He was suffering from lack of oxygen. It was time to go.

The day Tenzing and Hillary made it to the roof of the world was 29 May. Tenzing Norgay had never known his real birthday, so he decided that from now this great day would be it.

9

NEWS FINALLY REACHES LONDON

It's strange to think that when Hillary and Tenzing were photographing each other at the summit, nobody else knew they were there. In 1953 there was no easy way to send news from the top of a mountain. Even Colonel Hunt didn't know they had made it until they got back to camp. It would be four days before the public heard anything at all about their incredible achievement.

Several journalists were in Kathmandu following the story, but only James Morris, later known as Jan, of *The Times* newspaper had walked all the way to Everest. Morris had never been mountaineering before but managed to get to 6,700 metres and became the first outsider to learn that Tenzing and Hillary had reached the top.

Morris had to get this news to London as fast as possible and without any rival journalists finding out what had happened. To do this Morris typed out a message in secret code, scrambled down the mountainside and then paid a man to run more than 30 kilometres to the nearest radio station. The coded message was transmitted right away to somebody waiting for it in Kathmandu. This person then sent it on to the newspaper.

The secret message sounded glum and was meant to confuse anyone reading it without permission. Morris typed "SNOW CONDITIONS BAD. ADVANCE BASE ABANDONED MAY TWENTY NINE. AWAITING IMPROVEMENT". To those who understood the code it actually meant "Everest climbed. Hillary May 29 Tenzing".

The Times got the message and published its story on 2 June, but it wasn't front-page news. It happened to be Coronation Day in London, and people were far more interested in seeing the new queen, Elizabeth II, on her way to be crowned in Westminster Abbey.

It was several weeks before the adventurers finally arrived home to tell the full story of how they had made history in the Himalayas.

10

EVEREST TODAY

The *Guardian* newspaper heard about the difficulties the expedition had faced and reported that "it is doubtful whether anyone will ever try to climb Everest again". This turned out to be completely wrong, but it did

take another three years before a second group of climbers successfully reached the summit.

Today things are very different. Every year around 800 people try to climb Everest, with long queues sometimes forming near the top. Some of the climbers are as young as thirteen or fourteen. They come from all over the world and spend tens of thousands of pounds to do it, some of which is paid to the Sherpas. Nearly everyone who attempts to reach the summit is successful, but at least 300 have died trying. The death zone is still seen as one of the most dangerous places anywhere on Earth.

When someone dies at very high altitude, it can be too risky to recover the body or simply too expensive. This means that most of the dead on Everest are still trapped in ice or buried in the snow. Unfortunately their bodies aren't the only bad things people find on Everest these days.

Climbers often leave their equipment on the way down Everest as well as a lot of litter and other waste, including their poo. This has happened since Mallory tried to climb Everest, but the many thousands of mountaineers climbing it today mean that pollution has

become a major problem on Everest. Although efforts have been made to collect some of it, several tonnes still litter the slopes. What was once a beautiful and very special natural wilderness has become the world's highest rubbish dump.

People are trying to clear the worst of the rubbish and control the number of tourists. But Everest is in trouble – like many places around the world where nature is at its wildest and most spectacular. Mount Everest might be a very dangerous, very scary place, but it needs everyone who visits to respect it.